I0824575

PIECE BY PIECE

HOW STEPHEN SONDHEIM MADE MUSICAL PUZZLES COME ALIVE

By
ERIN FRANKEL

Art by
STACY INNERST

CALKINS CREEK
AN IMPRINT OF ASTRA BOOKS FOR YOUNG READERS
New York

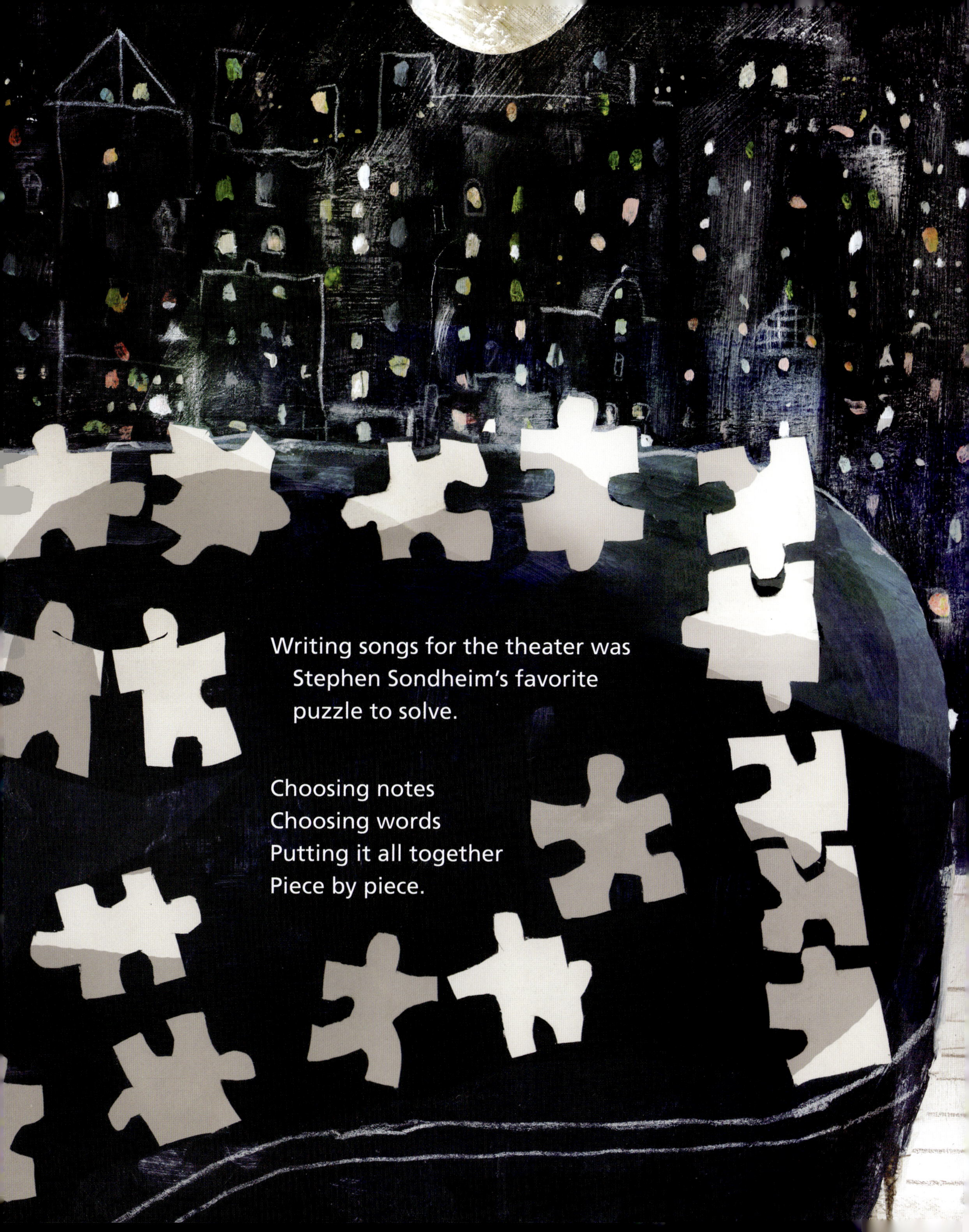

Writing songs for the theater was
Stephen Sondheim's favorite
puzzle to solve.

Choosing notes
Choosing words
Putting it all together
Piece by piece.

When the pieces fit together, the puzzle came alive!
Music and lyrics flying off the page and onto the stage
What could be more exciting!

Figuring out the pieces was hard work.
The kind Steve loved.

How does the character feel?

Is there a SOUND for such a thing?

Do the words BOUNCE with the music?

Do they RISE and FALL and SING?

It took *curiosity*.
The kind Stephen Sondheim grew up with.

As a boy, Stevie wanted to know *how*
things worked.
He put his hands on his father's
as they glided across the keys.
And watched the record player go round
and round
as show tunes filled their New York City
apartment.

Like most of his friends, Stevie took piano lessons.
He played the same songs over and over and gave recitals now and then.
It was all very ordinary.
But Stevie wanted something more.

One day, he saw a Broadway musical.
People chattering over *Playbills*.
The humming of the strings.
What was behind that big red curtain?
As the lights began to dim, Stevie held his breath . . .

. . . again and again and again.
How did they do it? he wondered.
How did they make the story come alive?

But while Stevie tried to figure out how things worked,
something else was falling apart.
Something Stevie couldn't solve.
His parents.

Stevie's life went through some rearranging.
Some pieces felt like they were missing.
But as he settled into a new school, other pieces helped fill the space.

He loved the order and the rules
and the organ as big as the moon!
Learning to play was hard, but to fill a room
with music and *surprise* . . . felt grand!
All those gadgets, all that sound.
Feet that barely touch the ground!

Before long, it was time for a different scene,
filled with *possibility*.
A new town, a new school, a new home—
just a bike ride away
from his new friend Jamie.

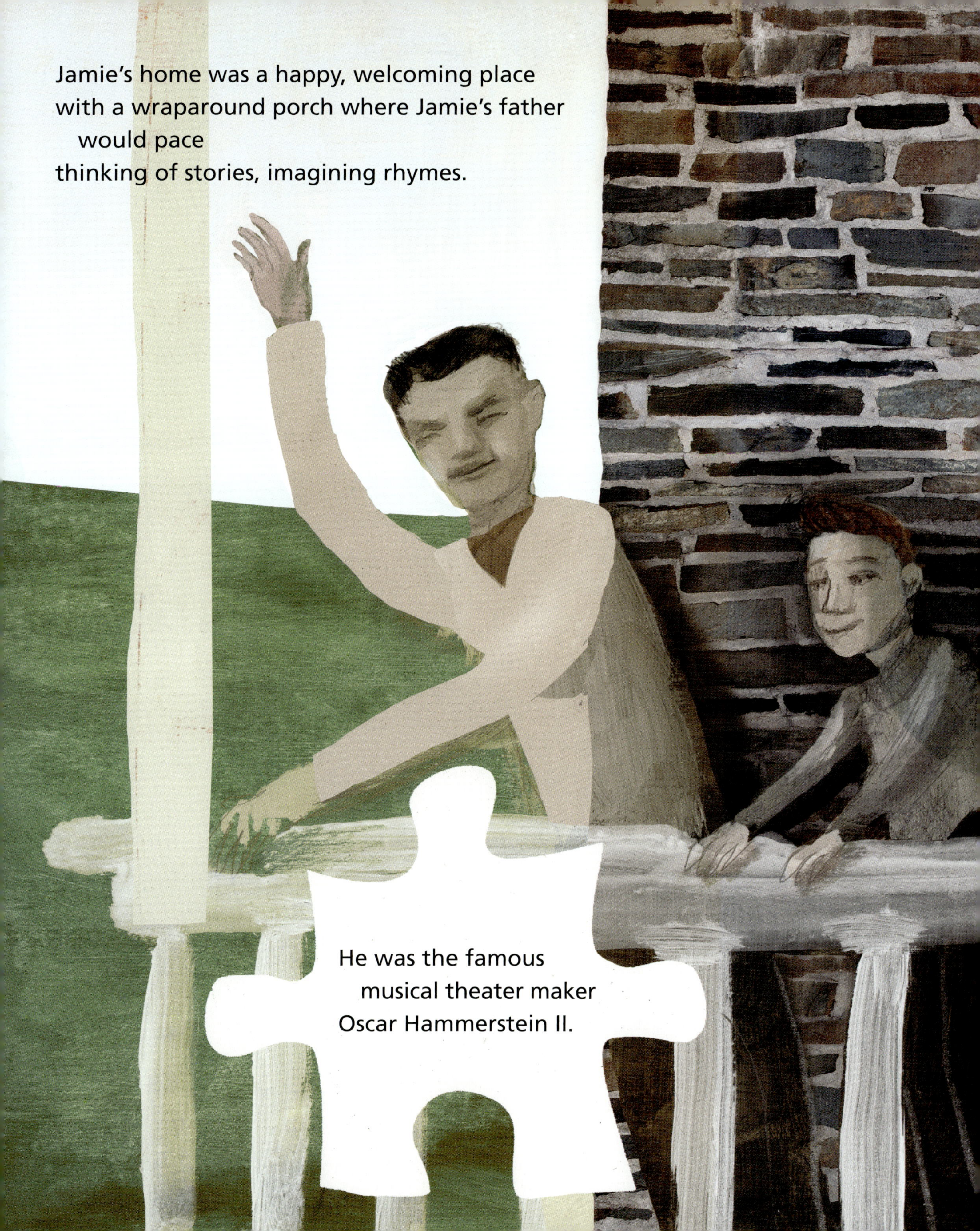

Jamie's home was a happy, welcoming place
with a wraparound porch where Jamie's father
would pace
thinking of stories, imagining rhymes.

He was the famous
musical theater maker
Oscar Hammerstein II.

Stevie's love for music and words was growing.

At the movies, he once stayed for the
second showing
to memorize a suspenseful score.

He learned languages and acted in plays.
But most of all, Stevie spent his days
figuring out how he could be
just like Oscar.

He decided to start big!
At just fifteen—Stevie wrote a musical.
Three acts, twenty songs, a cast of fifty on stage.
At his school, *By George* was all the rage!

He wondered if he might be
the youngest person to
write a show
good enough to go
to *BROADWAY!*

Certain that Oscar would think it was great,
Stevie was surprised when Oscar said it was *not* the best thing he had ever read.
But Oscar believed in Stevie.
If he wanted to learn, Oscar would teach him how.
The most important class of Stevie's life was starting NOW.

Oscar insisted the best way to get better was to practice putting the pieces together.

So that is exactly what Stevie set out to do.

But figuring out how wasn't easy.
Sometimes Steve wondered if writing music
was only hard for him.
Maybe other composers simply sat by windows
waiting for the perfect notes
to magically float in . . .

At college, Steve learned how artists usually begin.
The key to the magic was learning the craft.
Studying the greats.
Figuring out tricks.
And, of course, *practice.*

Steve watched others practice one summer
on Oscar's new show, *Allegro*.
It was *experimental*.
People daring to try something new.
Making mistakes. Figuring out *how*.
The musical was a flop, but that didn't stop Steve
from thinking . . .
Wow!

MAYOR

The more Steve learned, the more he wrote.
People started taking note.
Who was this young talent?

And lucky for Steve, he would soon be
collaborating on an exciting musical for *Broadway*!
Most of the roles were already formed.
Playwright for the book . . .
Composer for the score . . .
Choreographer for dance . . .
But for lyrics they needed one more.

Would he like to be the
lyricist and join their
creative team?

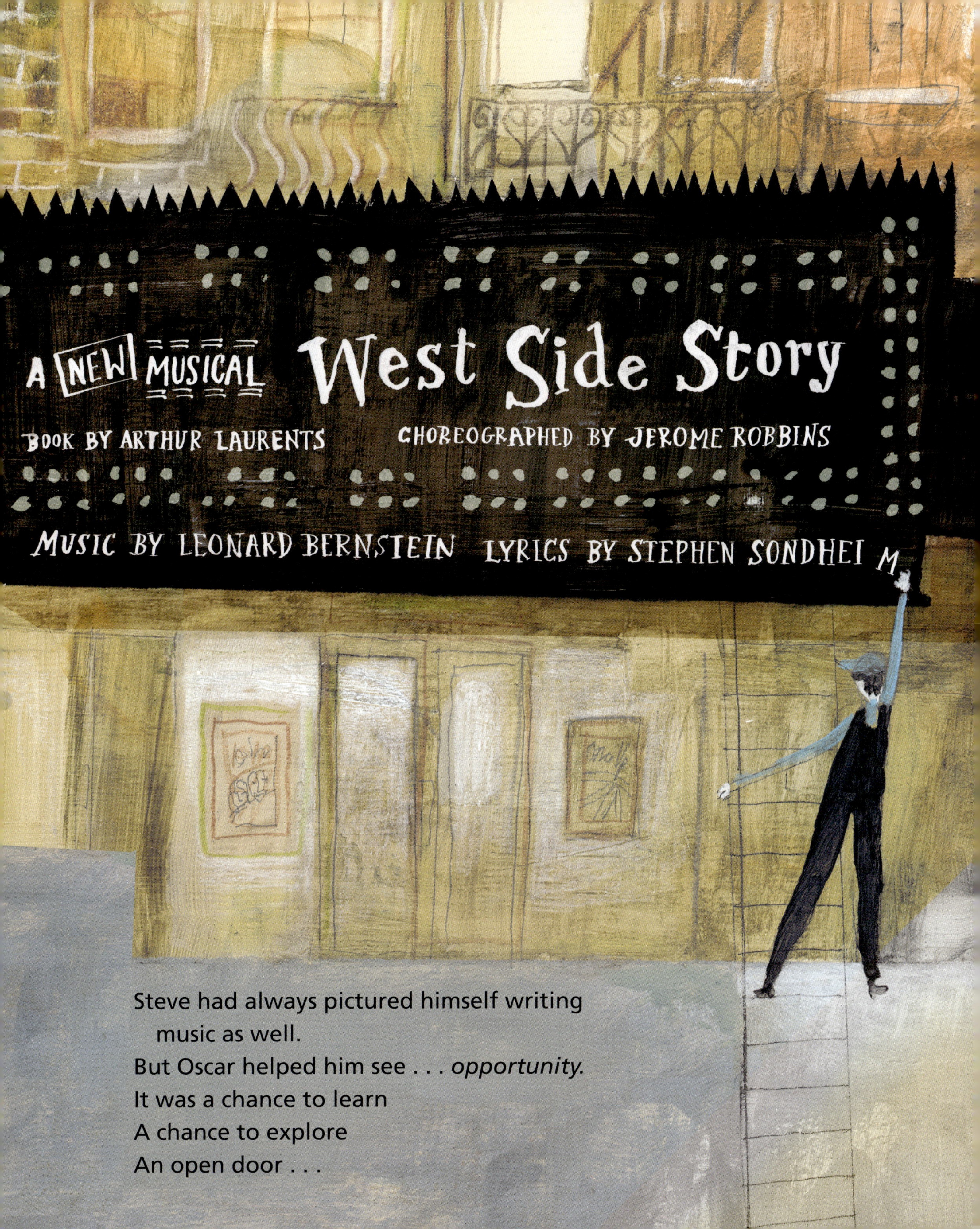

Steve had always pictured himself writing
music as well.
But Oscar helped him see . . . *opportunity.*
It was a chance to learn
A chance to explore
An open door . . .

His success with *West Side Story* paved the way
for more.
And with hard work, his vision soon came true.
Writing lyrics *and* music, too.
But Steve wasn't interested in writing songs
for just any story.
He searched for stories that spoke to him.
A story had to be different and want to
be something new.

A story had to have characters with complex feelings to explore. Characters like Steve who longed for something more.

Each new musical was a puzzle with a million pieces to put together.
Steve imagined each character in different places and different times,
Matching words and music to the details of their lives.

No detail was too small for Steve.

What is the sound for loneliness?
How did the Ancient ROMANS dress?
What chord shows TWO emotions at the SAME TIME?

Steve was taking audiences to extraordinary places,
Somewhere different every time.
But not everyone was ready for the unusual or new.
Once, when a musical closed quickly,
He wondered if he would start again.
Endlessly Inventive!
Melodious Score

But the thrill of the theater pulled him back in. So many stories still to figure out. So many songs yet to sing.

No matter the show, there was always *one* piece that *didn't* need figuring out.

It was exactly how Steve thought it should be.
Every show, a growing *family*.

Sometimes during a show, Stephen
Sondheim stood at the back and took
it all in.
He watched the puzzle unfold
piece by piece

And like magic,
put itself back together again.

AUTHOR'S NOTE

Weaving together pieces of Stephen Sondheim's life has been a joyful and profound experience. But in the spirit of Sondheim's life and work, it has also been complex. To fit the puzzle into a picture book, I chose the pieces that revealed themselves over and over again. The parts that were inevitable.

After his first break as a lyricist for *West Side Story*, he would go on to write the music and lyrics for more than a dozen Broadway shows. The wit, depth, and originality of Steve's writing were the heart of who he was and won him countless honors and awards, including eight Tony Awards—more than any other composer. From shows like *Company* with music and lyrics that matched the emotional complexity of *real* people to *Sweeney Todd*, a melodic musical thriller with rhyming gymnastics, Sondheim revolutionized American musical theater with his unmatched innovation. Collaboration with playwright James Lapine produced some of Sondeim's most soulful, artistic work including *Sunday in the Park with George*, which won the 1985 Pulitzer Prize for Drama, and *Into the Woods*, a reimagination of classic fairy tales woven together with unexpected twists. Steve felt that surprise was the heart of the theater, and together with the collaborators he so greatly admired, he gave the world much to devour.

At the heart of Steve's artistic journey was a passion for learning. He was filled with gratitude for the wonderful mentors and teachers who helped him on his creative journey. In turn, one of his greatest joys was the opportunity to give back in the same way. After his death, it became clear just how far-reaching his generosity and encouragement had been. Hundreds of performers took to New York's Times Square to sing his anthem "Sunday" from *Sunday in the Park with George*, and grateful theater-makers flooded social media with cherished letters of support and encouragement he wrote over the years.

Inspired by those outpourings of love and gratitude, I was reminded of how significant Stephen Sondheim's music and words had been to me. Once a college musical theater major, I cut my ambitions short with the realization that few of us would actually *make it*. But when I changed course, I felt like I was losing a piece of myself. Songs such as "No One Is Alone" from *Into the Woods* brought comfort while speaking to the sorrow I felt. It was this emotional ambivalence that spoke to me and that I now see defined Sondheim's work. Sometimes laughter, sometimes tears, but *always* the promise of an emotional journey that continues long after a song or show ends.

Like Steve, I am a storyteller filled with curiosity. I wanted to know how he transformed musical theater. How did he get his start? What were the pieces of his life that shaped him? What kept him moving on? To my great joy, I discovered the answer to a question at the heart of his work: *Why*? Piece after piece, Sondheim immersed himself in his craft for the *love* of it—even when it was hard. In doing so, he gave the world a gift that will live forever. Stephen Sondheim made us feel something *more*.

A young Stephen Sondheim (far right) next to his mentor Oscar Hammerstein II at Oscar's home in Doylestown, Pennsylvania

Steve rehearses for the Broadway musical *Merrily We Roll Along* (1981), with musician Edward Strauss and actor James Weissenbach.

TIMELINE

1930 Stephen Joshua Sondheim is born on March 22 in New York City.

1934 Begins taking piano lessons.

1939 Sees his first Broadway musical, *Very Warm for May*, and is thrilled.

1940 Attends the New York Military Academy when his parents divorce.

1942 Moves to Doylestown, Pennsylvania, with his mother and attends the George School. Favorite subjects include math and Latin. Frequents home of friend Jamie Hammerstein, son of Broadway lyricist and librettist Oscar Hammerstein II.

1945 Writes his first musical, *By George*, a spoof on his private school. Oscar's honest critique and suggested course of study inspire Steve to improve. He will later credit Oscar for his pivotal role as mentor and surrogate father. Oscar takes Steve to see his musical *Carousel*. Steve is moved to tears.

1947 Works as gofer on Rodgers and Hammerstein's musical *Allegro* during a college summer, igniting his interest in experimental storytelling.

1950 Graduates from Williams College, where he studied music and wrote several shows. Receives a prize for composition and continues to study with avant-garde composer Milton Babbitt.

1953 Works in Hollywood where he writes several scripts for the early TV comedy *Topper*.

1957 Makes his Broadway debut as lyricist for *West Side Story*. Within two years, he will work as lyricist on Broadway musical *Gypsy* (1959).

1962 Fulfills his vision of writing both lyrics and music with hit musical *A Funny Thing Happened on the Way to the Forum*.

1964 Learns that not every musical makes it big when *Anyone Can Whistle* flops.

1968 Constructs cryptic crossword puzzles for *New York* magazine. Often described as having a "puzzle mind," Steve wants to figure out how things work, driving his interest in games, puzzles, and creative work.

1970 Finds his artistic voice and revolutionizes the American musical with his collaboration with Harold Prince and George Furth on *Company*. Wins his first Tony awards the following year for Best Original Musical Score and Best Lyricist of a Musical.

1971 Writes music and lyrics for *Follies*, the most expensive musical ever produced at the time.

1973 "Send in the Clowns" from *A Little Night Music* becomes a pop hit and wins the Grammy Award for Song of the Year three years later.

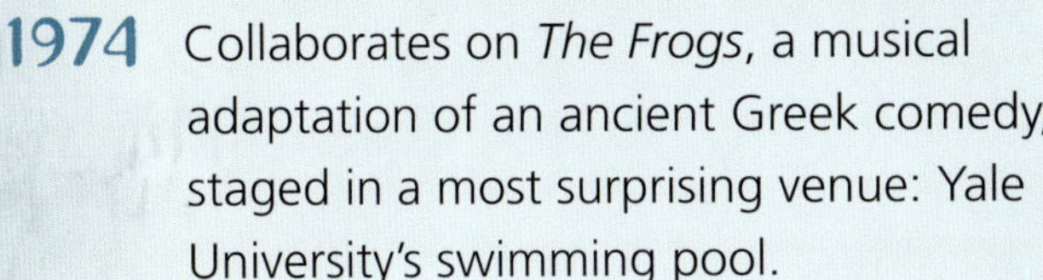

1974 Collaborates on *The Frogs*, a musical adaptation of an ancient Greek comedy, staged in a most surprising venue: Yale University's swimming pool.

1976 Writes music and lyrics for *Pacific Overtures*. Steve will recall "Someone in a Tree," as one of his favorite songs.

1979 Excites the theater world with musical thriller *Sweeney Todd: The Demon Barber of Fleet Street*.

1981 Feels discouraged when *Merrily We Roll Along* closes after a short run.

1984 Earns the Pulitzer Prize for Drama for his collaboration with playwright James Lapine on *Sunday in the Park with George*.

1987 Writes music and lyrics for *Into the Woods*, later adapted into a Disney movie.

1990 Writes music and lyrics for the controversial show *Assassins*.

Becomes first visiting professor of contemporary theater at Oxford University.

1993 Receives the Kennedy Center Lifetime Achievement Award.

1994 Writes music and lyrics for *Passion*, one of his most emotional works.

1995 Loses cherished personal items in a fire in his NYC townhouse.

1997 Accepts the National Medal of Arts from the National Endowment for the Arts.

2003 Writes music and lyrics for the musical comedy *Bounce*, eventually reconfigured as *Road Show* (2008). *Bounce* marks his final collaboration with renowned musical theater director and producer Harold Prince.

2008 Receives a Special Tony Award for Lifetime Achievement in the Theater.

2010 New York's Henry Miller's Theatre is renamed the Stephen Sondheim Theatre.

Receives an honorary doctorate of the University of London from The Royal Academy of Music.

Publishes *Finishing the Hat*, the first volume of collected and annotated lyrics. The second volume, *Look, I Made a Hat*, is published the following year.

2011 Inspires the Kennedy Center inauguration of the Stephen Sondheim Inspirational Teachers Awards.

2015 Receives the Presidential Medal of Freedom from President Barack Obama.

2017 Marries Jeff Romley. The couple split their time between NYC and Roxbury, Connecticut.

2021 Dies on November 26 in Roxbury. Broadway stars and fans gather in Times Square and sing "Sunday" in honor of his life and legacy.

Note: For a more complete list of Steve's accomplishments, explore the Stephen Sondheim Society, a UK-based charity dedicated to celebrating and studying the life and work of Stephen Sondheim.

SELECTED BIBLIOGRAPHY

All quotations used in the book can be found in the following sources marked with an asterisk (*).

Academy of Achievement. "Stephen Sondheim." February 17, 2022. achievement.org/achiever/stephen-sondheim/.

"The Art of Songwriting with Stephen Sondheim and Adam Guettel." YouTube, uploaded by the Dramatists Guild Foundation, April 28, 2020. youtube.com/watch?v=TofC3KD-h8M.

Barbaro, Michael, et al. "The Life and Legacy of Stephen Sondheim." Produced by the *New York Times*. *The Daily*, December 3, 2021. Podcast, 35 min. nytimes.com/2021/12/03/podcasts/the-daily/stephen-sondheim.html.

Breen, Kerry. "Broadway Legend Stephen Sondheim Took Time to Mentor Young Creatives. Here's What It Meant to Them." TODAY.com, December 30, 2021. today.com/popculture/broadway-legend-stephen-sondheim-took-time-mentor-young-creatives-here-t243972.

Collins-Hughes, Laura. "Cherished Words From Theater's Encourager-in-Chief." *New York Times*, December 3, 2021. nytimes.com/2021/12/01/theater/stephen-sondheim-mentor-notes.html.

*Eder, Richard. "Stage: Introducing 'Sweeney Todd.'" *New York Times*, March 2, 1979. archive.nytimes.com/www.nytimes.com/books/98/07/19/specials/sondheim-todd.html.

Everything Sondheim. everythingsondheim.org/.

Gross, Terry. "'On Sondheim:' The Musical-Theater Legend At 80." Produced by WHYY. *Fresh Air*, April 21, 2010. Broadcast, 46 min. npr.org/2010/04/21/124907187/on-sondheim-the-musical-theater-legend-at-80.

———. "Look, He Made A Hat: Sondheim Talks Sondheim." Produced by WHYY. *Fresh Air*, October 28, 2010. Broadcast, 46 min. npr.org/2010/10/28/130732712/look-he-made-a-hat-sondheim-talks-sondheim.

Horowitz, Mark. "Conversation with Stephen Sondheim." Library of Congress, November 21, 1997. loc.gov/search/?fa=partof:a+conversation+with+composer+stephen+sondheim.

*Kerr, Walter. "'Company': Original and Uncompromising." *New York Times*, May 3, 1970. nytimes.com/1970/05/03/archives/company-original-and-uncompromising-company-is-uncompromising.html.

Lapine, James. *Putting It Together: How Stephen Sondheim and I Created "Sunday in the Park with George."* New York: Farrar, Straus and Giroux, 2021.

———, dir. *Six By Sondheim*. HBO Documentary Films, 2014.

Max, D. T. "Stephen Sondheim's Lesson for Every Artist." *New Yorker*, February 14, 2022. newyorker.com/culture/the-new-yorker-interview/stephen-sondheim-final-interviews.

Overbey, Erin. "Sunday Reading: Luminaries of the Theatre." *New Yorker*, March 20, 2022. newyorker.com/books/double-take/sunday-reading-luminaries-of-the-theatre.

Pender, Rick. *The Stephen Sondheim Encyclopedia*. Lanham, MD: Rowman Littlefield Publishers, 2021.

Secrest, Meryle. *Stephen Sondheim: A Life*. New York: Vintage, 2011.

Sondheim, Stephen. *Finishing the Hat: Collected Lyrics (1954–1981) with Attendant Comments, Principles, Heresies, Grudges, Whines and Anecdotes*. New York: Knopf, 2010.

———. *Look, I Made a Hat: Collected Lyrics (1981–2011) with Attendant Comments, Amplifications, Dogmas, Harangues, Digressions, Anecdotes and Miscellany*. New York: Knopf, 2011.

Stephen Sondheim Society. "The Stephen Sondheim Society." sondheimsociety.com/.

Weber, Bruce. "Stephen Sondheim, Titan of the American Musical, Is Dead at 91." *New York Times*, November 27, 2021 (updated March 2, 2023). nytimes.com/2021/11/26/theater/stephen-sondheim-dead.html.

ACKNOWLEDGMENTS

All education is just about making people curious.
To get a child to be curious about everything would be . . . a thrill.
—Stephen Sondheim

To the writers whose work has informed my research and to my family and editorial team for helping me "finish the hat," I thank you. Special thanks to Rick Pender, award-winning theater critic and author of *The Stephen Sondheim Encyclopedia*, for sharing his expertise on this project. My deepest gratitude to Stephen Sondheim, for making the puzzle hard to figure out yet impossible to turn away from. What a joy it has been. May the story of Stephen Sondheim inspire curiosity in children young and old as it has in me.

A scene from Stephen Sondheim and James Lapine's musical *Sunday in the Park with George*, at Wyndham's Theatre, London (2006)

Album cover for the Original Broadway Cast Recording (1984) of Stephen Sondheim and James Lapine's musical *Sunday in the Park with George*, starring Mandy Patinkin and Bernadette Peters

Stephen Sondheim receives a standing ovation at the BBC Proms concert held at the Royal Albert Hall in London in celebration of his 80th birthday and his inspiring contribution to musical theater (2010).

Lin-Manuel Miranda leads an emotional tribute to friend and mentor Stephen Sondheim in Times Square. Sondheim's musical theater family came together in song to honor and remember the man whose music and words made them feel something more (2021).

For my grandmother Margaret "Peggy" Ritter
who always said "the piano is my friend." *—EF*

For my son Jake *—SI*

PICTURE CREDITS

Courtesy of The Rodgers & Hammerstein Organization, A Concord Company: 41 (top); Rivka Katvan: 41 (bottom); © Tristam Kenton. All rights reserved 2025/ Bridgeman Images: 46 (top); Bridgeman Images: 46 (bottom); PA Images / Alamy Stock Photo: 47 (top); Michael Hull Photo: 47 (bottom).

TEXT PERMISSION

Calkins Creek
An imprint of Astra Books for Young Readers,
a division of Astra Publishing House
astrapublishinghouse.com

ISBN: 978-1-6626-8095-3 (hc)
ISBN: 978-1-6626-8096-0 (eBook)
Library of Congress Control Number: 2025935721

First edition

10 9 8 7 6 5 4 3 2 1

Design by Barbara Grzeslo and Michelle Mayhall
The text is set in Frutiger LT Std.
The illustrations are done in acrylic, colored pencil, and ink.